Dogged Hearts

The Tupelo Masters Series

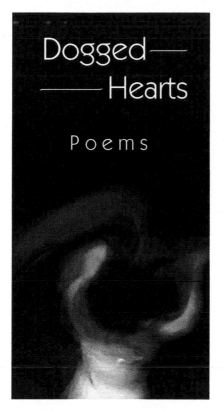

Dogged—
—Hearts

Poems

~~Ellen Doré Watson~~

For Barbara,
    Go sister — in any
voice that sends you!!

T|P   All warm
TUPELO PRESS   wishes
North Adams, Massachusetts

Santa Fe 2011   Ellen

Dogged Hearts
Copyright 2010 Ellen Doré Watson. All rights reserved.
ISBN-10: 1-932195-85-8
ISBN-13: 978-1-932195-85-9

Library of Congress Cataloging-in-Publication Data

Watson, Ellen, 1950-
  Dogged hearts : poems / Ellen Doré Watson. -- 1st pbk. ed.
    p. cm. -- (The Tupelo masters series)
  ISBN 978-1-932195-85-9 (alk. paper)
  I. Title.
  PS3573.A8523D64 2010
  811'.54--dc22

                                    2010013487

Cover and text designed by William Kuch of WK Design.
Cover photograph: "Iris 33" by Jack Spencer (www.jackspencer.com). Used with
permission of the artist.

First paperback edition: September 2010.
14 13 12 11 10   5 4 3 2 1

Printed in the United States.

Tupelo Press
P.O. Box 1767
243 Union Street, Eclipse Mill, Loft 305
North Adams, Massachusetts 01247
Telephone: (413) 664–9611 / Fax: (413) 664–9711
editor@tupelopress.org / www.tupelopress.org

Tupelo Press is an award-winning independent literary press that publishes
fine fiction, non-fiction, and poetry in books that are a joy to hold as well as
read. Tupelo Press is a registered 501(c)3 non-profit organization, and we rely
on public support to carry out our mission of publishing extraordinary work
that may be outside the realm of the large commercial publishers. Financial
donations are welcome and are tax-deductible.

NATIONAL
ENDOWMENT
FOR THE ARTS

Supported in part by an award from
the National Endowment for the Arts

For Della (you treasure) again and always

CONTENTS

DREAMING WE

DOGGED HEARTS

Hobbled by crab-apples underfoot, my body and I
flop into the car not altogether together and struggle
to find post-Yoga lithe. The back road offers a crone
—I can only use the word—*beholding* the dead deer
at her feet. Then a woman in a wheelchair whooshing
like breeze down a blue ramp. Chugging toward
school, a rail of a boy whose gait says *Any smaller,*
and I'd disappear. Fingerprints in motion, fleeting
disclosure. In town, a girl in the crosswalk—like her hips
are a gift. A mangy man outside the bank cradles
a guitar as if he just landed a whopping fish. How
inhabit this flesh we didn't choose? Love something.

DEAR RASH WORLD

AS WE SPEAK

Lilt, waft, balm, bruise—wet lilacs
leak their music. Thirty-some people

learn someone they love got slammed
between metal & mountain. When what's left

gets home, it's good to talk but not enough—
how can we put each other in the ground?

Rich, slick earth screams trench to the grocer,
mud-heaven to his grandson. Sound only travels

so far. How does it stop? Notes flutter, crystal
Post-its, ringing and ringing—and then what?

Perhaps sound is infinite though ears are not.
On someone locked in darkness, the idea of light

might fall, or would it instead rise down?
How can a wave / blossom / stallion / wound

be that lavish? Long hemmed in, burned
out, only glancing for decades, the cancer

is back in her back, exuberant. In the in-
between, above and beyond our knitting

and nattering, we're soothed by a singer,
even so-so. There is sky in her voice. And

that jumble of a tree throws out so many arms
its joy threatens the house as we speak.

YOURS, LENA

Between 6:10 and 6:24 the dream drained like a cup.
But as she unsheathes herself in morning dark, he lingers
as if real, this boy-child burrowed into borrowed warm.
She recalls how a younger self set out at a prance, singing,
but each time as she rounded the curve the gate banged
shut. Whose voice did she erase last night before listening?
Now nothing hammering but the hours. The boy is gone.
She imagines floating across the grass toward barn-smell,
dill makes a dry rain of its seeds. She could pull the sky
close and textured down around her shoulders, but what
a chill shawl it would make. Like bringing *miscarriage*
into a room. Like finding yourself on the same path again
and there's that slam, advance echo. Like pain waiting,
already yellow. 6:50. What is there she longs to topple?
Who to wake, what to build? She'll learn to forgive
the leaf-blower this day and to pray. Bless all who tend
a hurting blossom. And Dear Rash World so far outside
my window, oh fuck, may this third new nub of child live.

E. ZABALA, AGE 55, MULTIPLE FRACTURES, LOC

Perhaps he is Basque though he doesn't speak it now.
He's dreaming snow in skeins as they slide him clothed
into the scanner, ice chilly and bright. Outside he knows
night air weighs warm on skin. Thrown from a horse or
fallen from a ladder—how can he not care which?
Your name is Edur, you will remember yourself in time.
He's thinking he's on vacation from Captain Left Brain
with his pocket watch and brass words. This is like birds
loosened, he's fording a ragged river, then he's simply
shelling peas on a stoop. He's absorbing the gardenia.
When they reply, *no,* he is father to no one, he doesn't hide
his heavy cloak of grief. It becomes an apricot tree.
In his left hand, he finds a nettle; in his right hand,
a hand. There is some kissing left in his mouth.

LUCY'S WINDOW

New Year's Day breaks in her face,
blinding white, the world wanded
pretty and pretending it will last.
The bed's a bobsled hurtling through
a curving chute. Body insists
it's mind. Hers is thinking how any
other creature—when stuff flies at it—
must choose to seize or dodge. We're
the animal with option three: to frame.

CHOICE

Adam Foucault eats and eats and cradles
his eating. God knows if it will help, but
he's reading about his cortex, how it thinks
too many long-faced thoughts, whispers
to his hypothalamus to play along. He I.D.s
his very own bucket of reasons, scuffed-shoe
brain-paths deepening to ruts, ditches—and
goodbye pleasure. Everything suddenly sawdust.
He stands, he is winded. Mowed down. The sun
outside is a lie. The sun is not in his blood. What
would Freud do? (Smile.) He closes the book, stills
the static. His right mind says get dressed. Let each
gnawing desire have its 90 seconds, then let it go.
Adam knows about choice. He sets it on a plate.

ALONZO WHITE

She said the fetus is kicking and I didn't like
her calling it a fetus. Maybe it was mine, maybe
not, that's not where I'm coming from. It's ugly,
that word, like she means to keep it inside—not
real, not yet, we'll see about ever. Fetus, fetus,
fetus, in my head. I had no idea I didn't want that
kind of girl. OK, I know she gets the vote, and like
anybody sees me as a Dad, and I'm so not ready
to throw warm beer on my high, but when is it
that somebody signs up? Maybe I want to sign up.

NOTHING THEY SAID WAS GONNA MAKE ME HAVE THE BABY

They might as well turn it off. That bulrushes story—never
bought it. So, I'm chucking every bit of food down the toilet.
If I have to shrink, fine. Better to make it shrivel up now

than give it away once it's real—"it" keeps it not a kid,
not some little face stuck in my head. I'm OK with the aches,
I'm living off my smarts and my secret and how surprised

they'll be—till those pictures I saw got in my brain, African
kids all head and belly, and all I can think is ticks swollen
with blood and how long is this gonna take? I go online,

read about the stages: first you live off your fat, then muscle,
then organs, and that's what does you in, but me I'm not
suicidal, I just want my body back, and nothing anywhere

says starving makes the baby go away, just maybe retarded.
So it could be time to hit the Ben & Jerry's, but jeez, this dude
says going back to food is no picnic, either. These people in jail

who refused to eat—they force-fed them down a tube and
they freaking died, it's some chemical thing. "Hunger Strikers"
they're called, it's been going on forever, people not eating

to make a point, there's guys doing it right now, terrorists
or heroes who the hell knows, so I go back to the stuff
on fetuses, and that's when I'm a goner, wondering is it

the size of a kidney bean by now—and hey *keeping* the baby
would spite them more, so what if the world's fucked—and
long story short I'm heading for the kitchen and it's *my* bean.

NONE OF US IS DELIVERED CLEAN

Someone has to scrape off the cheese. Bo wonders
what still clings to him, from his inglorious birth
into alone? He's wet and flailing—if he let them,
his middle-aged arms would jabber the stinging air.
Who did she think she was—to push him out? His gut
clenches, the way this casts her as *mother*. Okay, say
it was as if she abandoned him on some doorstep—
yes, a simile provides distance—but how pathetic
abandon! Never mind. What mattered now was
the matter, the goo. And who would wield the rag?

SPEEDBOAT & CHAZ

His heart, startled buck at the sight of her
as a girl, writes an unremarkable script
on the monitor, hollow as he is, plopped there
in a johnny, his legs blasted off and left behind,
though he swears he feels his toes. Speedboat,
he calls her—all zip and shine. Now the cake
she made wilts on the tray, gift sits wrapped,
the ceiling claiming his interest in her wake.

Viewfinder the size of the sky, sky so vast
it dwarfs nothing, she backstrokes a retreat not
from the future of Chaz but the fact, each day's
gaze. She frets how never to go back inside.
Though she'd planned one day to leave him.
Though she would not have chosen spring.

SPEAKING OF REARRANGING

A sad, simple wish regarding one's own face
is one thing; entirely another when a fist
does the job. I feel like scrambled eggs, said
Junie the day she biked home to find a new
Mommy. Have you ever woken to discover
the claw-footed furniture has migrated,
cookbooks elbowed in among the fiction?
Perhaps boredom is thus proven universal.
Turning outward, pity the poor rocks. Not
the ones skipped into cool invisibility but
those bloodied by the verb "to stone." Like
us.

SPEAKING OF RICH

Rae-Ann is ranting that we rich are wrinkled
pleasingly like good linen. rain fills our ears all night,
in soft focus. Here underneath more than a leaf,
where storms get their names, days of rain demand
string quartets, high-nap naps, thought-mood. No
hunks of mountain come down. The dry in us (on
high ground) wants to knit, learn humid like clean
laundry sprinkled for the iron. Another taproot day,
and we think *gouache,* oil the sump pump, we sing
the sideways relation of sedentary to mud. For we
with roofs: water makes music, which wouldn't be,
without. A roof as an apparatus of appreciation! We
rich, swollen like wood.

EDITH'S ROOFER DREAM

Raw day, and I'm practically up in the clouds
next to some hard-hat hollering to another over
din of metal, smell of tar. The second guy grins back:
Verbal abuse is nine-tenths of the law! Swear to God.
Yeah, I guess I'm invisible—and plus somehow I know
at home on his dresser in a heap of change is the key
to a box he's terrified to open. Where does this stuff
come from? Meanwhile, a third man, heavyset, stoops
in the rubble, pretends to search for something, but
really he's worrying about how to fix the membrane
between him and the world, recently torn, letting stuff
leak in and out. *Whaddaya mean you don't want to be
a roofer?* booms a voice from above. Noon whistle
shrieks. All the guys on site grab their lunch boxes,
sit in a ragged circle. Remove their shirts, thermoses,
and Tupperware and—I kid you not—burst into tears.

MRS. NAPOLEAN GUAY HAS AT ROBERT FROST

So he parrots his father sometimes—that doesn't make
my husband wrong, any more than fine phrases make
our Yank neighbor good at the land. All spring-eager,
he loves the big broken teeth or loaves or whatever
he calls them strewn between us. Frost having opened
the gap, he rings us up. He thinks us pine-dark and rote,
innocent of innocence of apples, when our ramrod firs
could overtake his orchard. He takes his axe to heart.
My husband makes axe-helves. Shoulders a boulder and
says it again, the famous line about fences. We've not seen
the inside of that man's house. We don't believe in elves
is what I'd say. Look at them both, here in my kitchen,
snake-sure. One all work, the other playing at it. Boys.
I rock toward fire. I am the mystery in the room.

ANGRY IVY ON PLANET CHANCE

On the day chosen to—what the hell—leave everything
to chance, Ivy wakes at first light, on account of the catbird,
and asks fate to dispatch the foul thing at the outset, then sees
the flaw in her thinking and repents. Damn. Repentance being,

well, inappropriate in a chaotic universe. *God,* would she ever
—another slip of the tongue—get this right? She wanders
from the maze of her thoughts to her smart red car. Something
big is burning in Whately. This week the marquee out front

of the evangelical church claims: "God made me to love you"—
which elicits a chuckle, presumptuous lie that it is, yesterday
today and tomorrow. A ball plonks off the windshield, she
panic-brakes: where's the kid? No kid. Even the terrifying

everyday probabilities are up for grabs. What about statistics
—on Planet Chance are they all of a sudden obsolete? Genetics?
The number of LSD trips that puts a brown-eyed female at risk
for schizophrenia is one-tenth that for a blue-eyed one with no

brown-eyed gene. What about forgiveness? Will her husband
go on claiming women think they can change anything? It's all
getting too fuzzy and she needs to pee. There is always glass
everywhere. No glue and no sure reflection. Chance allows her

neither to turn around nor to drive *foot-to-the-floor-right-on-by.*
She scrunches her cheeks alternately, first only the blue eye open,
then brown. Dexterous as a coin toss, she'll gas with the left foot,
brake with the right. If she's alive when the car stops, God knows

it'll be tomorrow.

LEW'S LATE LOVE

The fourth month flowers waxy and small.
Grief is like sleeping in water, he thinks. Like
throwing light onto the smallest stone. It is
like scolding a doorjamb for crushing a finger
in third grade. Her finger. Now in the ground.
The same one she fractured flying off a treadmill
the day her first husband walked away. Why
these vignettes that long preceded him, now,
his ninety-first day without her? Long week after
week in a world now narrow. A runner instead
of a proper rug. If he could stand her there, across
the disbelieving room, he'd ask, all sheepish, how
she was doing without hunger. He can hear her
smile: "Look at the lake. Tell me I can't have it."

FIRST SIGHT

A blind woman—who by some miracle can
no longer hear the far stream spilling down
the far hill because for the first time her eyes

are filling—stands fixed and faint at her window:
the barn drawn so close, the cat—how could he
have pinned between his paws at this moment

some poor creature?—what would death
look like instead of smell? But it's only bark—
a bit of tree!—and trees from all sides assemble,

long-fingered bare hands grasping for sky.
The clouds say nothing of what's behind them,
the way they glare down on the amazing

semi-transparency of ice. Her eyes are hot
and hungry for house-bound things, memorized
by touch, so whole now they hurt: the saxophone

aglow on the rug, the party the afghan makes
on the bed, her own features aslant in a watery
mirror: recognition ringing in her fingers—terrain

of mother! Oh, petticoat waterfall, loud window:
that never-seen curve of lip, those smooth teeth,
this mouth—yes red spurt of bird in sudden sun—

SPEAKING OF SPLITTING IN HALF

It could be one of us, or the two of them. Hysterical or historical, that moment's a clean part down the scalp of something huge, lice on one side, frosting on the other. We are so busy splitting things: coconuts, hairs, atoms, noggins. There's a mental hospital in Rio with a museum of patient art, post-lobotomy: every single piece a sphere newly fissured. Children know the good little me and the bad; they just don't realize that they win either way, for a while. Except the few who are sent hurtling back up the chute. Do people kill kids to kill kids—or to hack open the parents as someone hacked them?

SPEAKING OF VICARIOUS

Mother says what's a couple of mimosas among friends, sits murderous on the couch, seam-ripper at hand and knows she will watch, instead of using it. Dix is the red velvet cake her mother doesn't know how to make. She is fleet on her feet. People learned the word insinuate watching her glide. She starts as a bright painted object and then your eyes do tricks: suddenly no edges, all breath. You know how they say a drunk has to bottom out to see straight? You know how they say there's an afterlife?

BEGONIA WAS HER NAME-O

She refused on sunny days to leave the room
between ten and twelve-thirty: transfixed, she
permitted nothing between her and the window.
The rest of the time the floor grate yawned,

infusing her with dread even as it flooded the room
with warmth. She'd sooner devour a rotten onion
than look at that thing. *All orifices must remain sealed!*
The tape talked of neuro-transmitters and it troubled

her that she'd forgotten how to sing—or maybe
she was by instinct avoiding activation of anything
below the neck. For two months she'd been faithful
to her vow not to speak. One month left. Humming

was okay (wordless, in the head). She saved up crusts,
ritually dropping them into the right boot in the closet
because the toe housed a mouse. That would explain
the noises smaller than she was in the night. Wildly

unfair was what she thought about the prohibition
against candles, when they could simply outlaw matches,
could they not? Against her own rules, she put silent words
to her hum: *Pray me a candle.* This pleased her: 3 a's, 2 e's,

and not one repeated consonant, yet was it grave enough
for her first utterance when March 5 rolled around?
Next, she settled on: *You found me so* [beat] *slowly,*
starting and ending with y, and all those lovely o's, but now

she had her doubts. The snow was shrinking fast and dirty.
One day, after a long stint in the window scrubbing the word
skull from her forehead, she recalled the dictum to be "measured."
Yes, she thought. *The sadness in this child is the size of Arizona.*

FIREFLIES AT THE ALTAR

The air here does kind of taste like lemons,
thought the boy in the hammock, swaying
his way to the future. The bride would be

dead within the year, everyone in their finery
knew this. Which was why she brought the boy
along, nestled in yellow petals that trembled

with each footfall. She'd invented him exactly
three days after diagnosis, whispering
to her overies as she fingered childhood photos

of the man waiting now on the alter, all full
of this wedding and the way he would hold her.
The gathered ones gaped at the gray of her,

the size of his love. She cared less for its heft
than for his knowing how to tame it: sex,
the purest kind of barely-touching. Now

her body was in her dress, the ring was sliding
onto her finger. Everyone watching her become
"one" with the man who couldn't come along.

Fire raging in the room above his head, the boy
dreamed he was brushing his teeth with fireflies,
which were not hot, but yellow, dry, and feathery.

SUDDENLY SOLARES

Dolores's innards stewed, sawing back and forth.
Ever since Father kicked open that door: he never
laid hands on her but his feet. Door never shut right
after that, and her insides acquired barbed wire.
She knew not to ask about her long-disappeared mother,
or why the neighbors flocked to their door with offerings,
like he was king: fresh eggs, afghans, lush tomato plants.
It felt as though they trailed through her gut to get there—
and they got to walk away. Until suddenly Dolores looked up:
an urgent "V" of geese froze their honking flight right over
her head and she knew her path would be the slap of shoes
pounding the night toward sunrise. Well, the geese part
she added later to the tale she'd spun that dazzle of a day
when Solares decided to remove the pain from her name.

THROWN FREE

Bleeding beside an exploded headlight, how silly
to be thinking of her cancer, looking for her purse.
But now she could see the face inside the oncologist's
face, her husband's shoulder—doors reducing to windows,
words to wind. We are as blind as need be. What if
she'd been faithful? Let him keep the damn monkey?
Why the holy hate for her mother? We brace for cold,
fly to greet each hotspot (different soundtrack, same
menu), until X. We all have our tipping-points. Neurons
leap the ditch, cortex floods with ones and zeroes in one
or another combination. Oh, how memory bobs and pops.
Swimming to her now, welcome as a blanket, the clang
symphony of three dead dishwashers flung off the truck!
Some rehearse the lip of wave, others look into the water.

UPRIVER

Baker points himself upriver, threads the road
toward home, where neither old nor new love
fizzes or chats or clatters. To the left, machines
noise the pines; to the right, the late light

tears across fallow fields after anything shiny.
No longer anyone's *how was your day* he is
twice himself. Nothing comes screaming at him.
Brush huddles in too-velvety dusk. He wishes

it dangerous, then not, remembering someone's
cheekbone shattered like fine china thin under
earthenware skin. Familiar hillsides are knitting
their shrouds. Stepping out into baby bullfrog racket,

he's wrapped in their low song, the pond's mouth
open to the stand of cherries—trees that sicken cows
and look down on a dozen skinny chirpers, inchlings
soon to be food. All he needs is permission to burn.

SPEAKING OF SUN

Tess is aiming for full color, feeling sepia. Be not alarmed, says her lesser half, in half light, armed to her yellow teeth. Believe me, I've seen worse, says her borrowed optimism. You're kaput, says her thumping chest. She imagines her best thoughts wincing, pictures a stranger who offers each thought a tall glass of water. They drink themselves liquid and run through her veins singing thanks straight to the heart. That's the flushed face her better half puts on.

BAKER & TESS

IN THE AIR

She hacks at daylilies, all
common and ruthless. He
tap-taps silver slivers
into spongy sills, spills
nothing. Beads of sweat
gather under her breasts,
his hatband, but they are
far from physical. Far off
the phone bring-brings.
Nobody moves. They look
around, as if a shrub
were a merciful thing.

SHE SCREECHES AT CROWS

That article called them cheeky—
I'm all for cheeky, but this black
male racket scribbles meanness
on the morning. He *watches* them
is all. My outburst shuts them up
for five seconds of breakfast.
I worship the drilling shower
blasting me back to days I'd wake
to sounds difficult to discern. No
wonder they call them a murder.

HE WATCHES THEM

At first I think they're fighting for food,
but this fuss is play: when one drops a small
something from the high white pine, they all dive
for it. Their midair scrapping-and-screeching dissolves
my scowl at her silence, sends me to Google, then to shame—
not because these oil slicks with mouths (both predator and prey
who mate for life, shove food down baby throats every ten minutes,
whose young babysit for generations) are legally shot out of the sky—but
because I think only of me when I read: "Nests are tragedy waiting to happen."

SHE'S ACTING

as though I am the discussion she wants
to avoid. Would I weren't necessary.
(I am not necessary.) Would she couldn't
see me. (She sees me through blood-
colored glasses.) Would I were not
parenthetical, or she not skimming.
(She isn't even skinny.) It says here
wood absorbs us, all our oils. What about
when it's left to drift, shorn of touch, strewn,
drying, that kind of furniture. I am tabled.

WHAT TESS WANTS

A wooden bowl, fragrant oil, and a good
half hour. Cello to accompany a careful task,
not one draught. Please, not a forest but a bevy
of single trees. Oh and I want him far away
or at least his anger. Like that voice that says
we'll be erased when we hang up, I wish he
would. I wish he'd stop painting the house and
discover color. I want my arms heavy with sun
like boughs with snow and everyone's heads
to stop hurting. I want a weeded house,
an ocean a month, time with my spice grinder.
I'd like one day someone new to make me supper.
I don't want to feel marinated or married, but
yes, one flower—wild—worthy of a vase.

DIMINUET FEMININA

Did I take hue for true? How much did I chalk up simply
to the spinning years? Without my fingers' knowing,
a knitting—a wanting taking shape, and—bam—
what I imagined wanting next was else,
was out. Like stones, think of them,
sub-color, working their way up
through—well—everything.
Bright wet meets sun meets
wind, shine takes itself
away, and the stones
go dusty and subtle
and something
I need.

FAULT

None of it was my doing.
All of it was. She needed
a sea change. We gave away
the dog, flew to the new.

Same, same, same, was all
she sang, answer to every
blessed question. Sorry,
sorry was my refrain, surely

she'd change, like weather.
Remember Quepos, I asked,
how the cement floor rolled
and pitched and stayed whole?

Yes, she said. I am the sand
scattered across it. Sparse,
irritating, unable by nature
to hunger, or be amazed.

NIGHT MIRROR

All night she sat at the silver window deciding
whether the glass revealed the world's face or
her own. She knew perspective—pine needles
softened to feathers at the right distance, new
whetstones sharpening old aches into blades.
This night something on one side or the other
was powering down—whether in a clutch
of her cells or across town. Two hands thirsty
in her lap. The river lapping at the road's
toes, its current dark and thin as her blood.
The gorgeous forgery of self-love—as if
the glass in its wisdom could give herself back.

WHAT KEPT AFTER HIM

What kept after him was *nub,* what she
    —who knows when—had become.
She disappeared into her clay more
    and more, ashy to the elbows,
the wheel's thwap and hum singing
    up from the barn through summer's
white hot window. Invisible, he emerged
    from the river, a huge fish in his arms
that for the first time asked why. For
    once, he worried her distance, not his
ache. Neither of them saw he loved her now
    without swagger, frontally, new in his age.
Meanwhile everything green slowly broiled

    into orange, then brittled into ice,
the path to the barn no longer choked
    but naked. She in the barn layered up
but still cold, the house cold without her,
    and him left brushing the dog, the fire
like crumbs. If she came up to the house
    it was with clean hands now, business
-like. If she had a lover, he thought
    better to rub her feet than to ask who
or what sex, yet. What kept after him
    was *bun,* by which she used to mean
honey. Morning had given him a river.
    All he wanted was for her to drink.

WOMAN LEANING TOWARD THE DOOR

1. Because He Is Nothing If Not Constant

Zealous will, disarm.
Zealot self, un-self.
Because years, because
Oh! And what I owe—

where are my open arms?

2. Because He Is Nothing If Not Constant

Been we two. Been we tied:
(Been with child, child be glue.)
Be we three, I have tried.
One is who I am.

He wants why, thinks me cold.
Has his arm around my neck
and doesn't even know.

KNEELING MAN

No ring in a teensy box to fish
from his pocket. He'd almost like
to erase that moment now but

instead fishes his wedding band
from where it rolled in the sawdust
while he fiddled with the clamps.

Christ, he'd like to erase even
her scent. What a fool, he thinks,
admiring the marquetry, the grain,

this fine gift he just now knows
he will never give her, remembering
splatter of wine on white tablecloth,

sweet teeth inside a smile. He had felt
so—yes—debonair. But she looked,
instead of pleased, triumphant.

EVERYTHING HE EVER HAD THAT HAS DIED

Father. Mother. Numberless creatures—flushed,
tossed, or gently fed to the backyard, depending
on how furred or expressive. Totemic objects
of affection, human and otherwise. Cars, toasters,
washers hauled away. Umbrellas traded for hats.
His bridge game. Only two watches—he stopped
believing in them. Two marriages. Friend after
friendship. Ambition. His looks, agnosticism, not
his anger. His generosity—but not toward strangers
(danger is familiar). The bleeding heart by the stoop.
Memories (zip-locked, tossed). Every bike he ever
owned. The chicken house. Peripheral vision. Tears.
Gregariousness. His fighting fish. His planting hands.

AS IF LOVE

were cool and simple, jade against skin.
As if early gifts could negate late inattention.
The way she just stands there, tippety
with counterweights, hands jammed in pockets.
As if even my seeing them would be a thanks
I don't deserve. As if her wrists, bare as the day
I pinned them to the table, and oh her mouth,
never-ready, like the elbow she used to offer me,
to steer her smiling into the sea of smiles.
As if trust didn't sail in both directions.

AS IF IN COMPLETING A SENTENCE
THERE WAS DEATH

He was an inconstant father
to his own ideas, loving,
then brutal. Months to proclaim,
cajole, embroider, then

beat down, disown.
The hollow in him insisting
on itself, the pattern
so protracted and full

of turnings it almost amounted
to beauty. And all his life, sex
the blindfold, the punctuation
so loud the road's sameness

stayed veiled. If years begin
by adding masks, they end
by removing them. This song,
that blueprint, drowned like kittens

by his own hand. His dick gone
lazy. Interruptions no longer
the coin of his realm but the matter,
the what, the baby after shaken baby.

HOW HE KNOWS

Clay baby-claw, ye olde pointing finger sign,
hand tree holding her many rings, palm-reading
kit, five-fingered switch-plate, spoon rest, child's
hand-print permanent on the dashboard, fridge
magnets, hand candles, fist-on-a-chain, anatomy
book, photos of hennaed hands, porcelain palm
for spare change, ancient mannequin hand
with crazed skin, five pairs on ear-wires—no
surprise she worships palm trees, and studied sign
language—if someone were to cook the meat off,
strip one to bones, she would pay cash, place it
proudly with the others, yet no matter how hard
I try, how soft I touch, she can't suffer mine

FLOOD, ACCORDING TO HER

You are like a leaky row boat pretending
to be a raincoat. I am straight-forward:
self-confessedly undependable because
my right arm overrules my left, just like
my brain. Life within a fortress within
a life in an arc of motion, oh Russian doll.
How to be the years we have? I'm thinking
of love. I'm planning to make up the truth:
this end-stage sunset, that baby landscape.
I'm thinking of laying down slabs of stone
across the lawn, big feet of heaven, whole
kingdoms. *Feng Shui* my way: a cadre
of rubber alligators to protect my door.
It's not as though we can pick up every
shell on the beach, but there's often
something nesting in the nest of the bird
in the hand. One day I just stepped out
of the boat. Relief like a flood I tell you.

FLOOD, ACCORDING TO HIM

You don't understand limits. Visiting cities
with high water marks, you marvel and

flounce on, not a minute's stillness to absorb
all that's been swamped, what it's like

to be assailed. You're playing solitaire.
I'm dreaming backlit backgammon, bigger

back yard—and you're the goddamned
wave. You try to avoid my mouth. You fill it.

LEFT MAN TALKING

Bless the brain, god-damned mustard seed,
conveyor belt, valet
laying out impermeable shirts, reasons
I'm meant to wear, to eat, supposed roads
away from beckoning wreckage

Bless is curse is remember forget

One minute it's *stupid prick, lie down dead she's gone*
and the next, *here, boy*

What dope would choose a woman with an iron mind
She didn't mind
She gleamed

Don't say she, she wouldn't say why
She hated parrots, indecision, the word skull
Don't

Don't blame x for y
or fog or feet
getting carried away with themselves she's gone

Bless oh curse this vacant
house my heart
Weapons there are everywhere
I have no hands

HE WANTS TO KNOW *WHY?*

Because the road washed out or I wasn't on it
Because I took a fork in my sleep or woke up
Because I stuck it into him (he would say "us")
and hurled all the cutlery off a cliff I'm eating
with my hands grease to the elbows marrow
in my teeth something not his running down
my leg in my head because I was washed out
took woke stuck hurled eating running

WHAT TESS NEEDS

Tess needs to weed. Less appetite, more
aperture; old roses, fat thorns. White space,
not white noise. She needs to turn her pockets
inside out, hum the tune of the empty basket.
She knows who's talking to whom, third person,
second: *You. You need to lure whole hands, sleep
on sand, rhyme-y and slack-mouthed under the moon.*

MAN HOLDING HIS BREATH

Why is the waffle iron still here?
You're the garage sale queen, you
filmed the windows with smoke.
You have abandoned your shampoo.
That sick-sweet frozen puddle
of a candle makes me think lesion.
Come back for your slightly moldy
art books. You are an encyclopedia
of smells. The tub bears traces
of coconut and lemongrass. I
taste you. You live in my lungs.

BEYOND

As in beyond reason, i.e. past, farther than him.
Further along, down the track, possibly off
the track, as in off-track betting, or bedding down
elsewhere, as in outside faithfulness, beyond
fondness, beyond finding, as in retrieval, lost
to the great beyond, as in God if you're beyond
belief. At the far side of anti-parental, surpassing
source, in excess of, over and above, later than,
as in my late husband, not that he's dead, just
former, an old formulation, past elation, distant
relation, beyond comprehension to the point of:
Be Yond, as in get thee yonder, i.e. out of my sight,
yonder, away at a distance beyond distance, any-
where I am *not,* as in *with you.* I'm beyond that.

LAST TANGO

Argentina can have you, Tess,
for all I—   *I care!*

You said it   *but it's time we speak as one voice go each*
spit swallow bellow   *our graveled ways*

If you were rain you'd be hail   *Yes but proud and you mist*
Better than rain inside   *which you think Zen*
                                          —ha it's a nap

Heady leak not speaking   *Better than spacious waste*
                                          needy feed me

You went from electric to ballistic   *You from game to lame*
and disappeared   *into your little bits of wood*

You crutch loving it so much   *But also your husbandry*
                                          old shoulder

Then cold untold
what in the world
                                          Exactly the world
                                          is what aced you

You iced me
                                          Despite your cheek your cous cous
                                          your rusty tenor
spliced me   *it wouldn't work to nice you*

and so my bleeding out   *My blade my salve how both*

My tourniquet horizon   *Now said and sad*

and done   *for all we*

care—   d

DREAMING WE

DEATHDAY

In the last 3 days I have killed 138 ladybugs.
Oh, I was methodical and unrelenting
Fool suicide, their scheme to winter
chez moi. A year ago my mother
was eating her last gruel and
learning to stop. Impossible,
watching her gates close,
that I ever fit inside—or
that she pushed me out.
Knowing comes, as I
flush the bitty red
bodies down:
it's me that
I mourn.

TICKS OF FLAME

Ticks of flame lick my wrists, ankles, knuckles—
a molten flaring from the inside, which is where
half our danger launches, lunches, sets up camp.

How convenient—a diagnosis (or lack of) to worry,
just as I was about to tackle a stranger's urgencies,
gather an array of flailings and fractures waiting

to be loved from afar. Dear irony, I was just thinking
I haven't paid enough attention to shivering leaves,
wet stones, inevitability. I was trying to nix my

my. But ten to one, I'd have prattled on as usual
about the lover in the wings, or waxed wry or wise
about oh my dear ones, their proppings and upswings

and scraps of lovely. Instead, I'm reduced to—surprise!—
living in a body. But I'm so far from the paraplegic
on the radio who refused to blame his body or to envy

ours: *Look how hard it works,* he said tenderly. Me,
I'm a ragged, blaming scarf, riveted on her stitches,
chagrined to be scared silly, ticked at the ticks of flame.

WHATEVER THIS IS

I'll scale the steps and cross the smooshed-crab-apple-
infested grass, but I refuse to clamber down the bank
unless the river is known for its stones. Useless
distinctions like this I have lately clung to—or

shall I say lately designed? Indecision is legion here
in the (aging) meat of my years. I've established
that the chaise is not curtseying to the birdseed bin
any more than the rags are cozying up to the pile

of windows, which it turns out are feeling neither
displaced nor blue. But I swear that slug stood up
and made a shadow, which, while miraculous, possibly
even purposeful, is not sufficient to the human evening

any more than sweeping before sleep the dropped needles
from the walk. Just look what's happening to my house—
its skin set right and bright—as I turn to lumber.
Memories almost as gone as the tiny clay houses that once

nestled the rock wall, which is to say not gone. Flickering.
Gravity! Get the hell away from me sings a twenty-something,
sings (I pretend) the phlox I didn't deadhead, the buoyant
ground cover, the mess of leaves toast-dry, unruly.

Opening into risk is for yesterday and tomorrow—
the other side of whatever this is, this chain (of my own
making?), which is at least not the splintered ladder
left sprawled and numbing in the wettish grass.

THE PERSON YOU CANNOT LOVE

The person you cannot love is your mother
—is you, for that thought—mother of what?
Is that bundle of string bean limbs
and searingly soft skin your mother?
Asking whether she's your mother

if she doesn't know she's your mother
is like asking whether she's your mother
if she's dead. She is moved from bed
to chair to bed. A kind, paid hand dabs
her teeth with little pink sponges on sticks

and you let her be so dabbed. Are you mostly
nowhere to be seen because she doesn't see?
Do you avoid those pale mismatched pupils
for her loneliness or yours? A year ago,
if you planted a kiss on her cheek, her mouth

would pucker, but now her response to touch
is to startle. She is so far from speech, how dare
you feel stranded? Her verbs are reduced to cough,
moan, sometimes swallow—but what about those
of your heart? Exhorted to commune, you moisten

her lips, look into the abyss, think the word *bored*.
She sags a ragged sigh. Her crusted lips yammer.
You can't answer them and you have no Lord,
so you call on hers. Lord, you say, still dry-eyed:
Please. Make her dead so I can love my mother.

BEFORE SHE GOES

Take the idea of her *gone* and stuff it—
down, sharp, deep where it will trouble you
in ways you can't measure. No one's outlawing
anything but the daily. To translate yourself
from featherbed to couch throw, you will need
reference works, nerve, and native speakers.
If it could think mid-span, your heart would heave.
Desolation is on the launch pad and everything
is more biological than you pegged it. Put no faith
in worship, nor in the scholarship of canyon
but in the canyon itself. It's yours now: wild, milk-fed
river, starry walkabout, birth-juice of bedrock.

KNOT IN NIGHT SKY

Many-shouldered, singular, neither
lithe nor husbanded, the copper beech
looms, above all a knot, above all things
rooted, ground-bound. Its leaves are little
clingers, whispery bronze lingerers
that leave it only briefly naked. O, my
mutant armful of arms, frenzy of reach
and choice. You roil in stillness. Are we
landing, or taking off? Both, you say,
by seeming inaction, mere thrust. What's
a tree to do? Or a woman, similarly
scarred and stolid and unable to fly?

GHAZAL FOR SHAHID

So, if there's a God, does He comfort or jeer first?
Write the poem backward, you said: put the fear first.

Coaxing hundreds of *ghazals*—real ones—from us,
Who can say whether you wowed or endeared first?

"Whoever you are, I depend on your message."
Call Shahid, and that's what you'd hear first.

Hands in earth, late sowing daffodils, I think how
You drove a *Stanza,* became a citizen here first.

Urdu poetry, Dante, Peer Gynt—near the end
You remembered things learned in Kashmir first.

What's gone to unknown we must knowingly treasure.
(I'll not forget Zeke, almost-son, who was mere, first.)

Ellen, you said—climb what you don't know and *go.*
Belief is a dance on earth: whatever you do, be here first.

BE HERE FIRST

I don't *know my trees* but I know *my* trees.
Their angling for what has spurned them;
their spitting and drooling, the battered

crocuses at their feet. We share the roofline,
the cesspool, I'm responsible for all that salt.
From my stone stoop I watch the lilac's sun-

starved horizontal heroics, the still-naked
redbud shrugging off bitty unlit lights.
Neglect leans back on the lawn chair.

Must we dislike ourselves to change?
Sick of every other part of me, I approve
my hand slobbered by the horse's jawing

a hacked apple. I say fear is behind our
everything. Or brazenness, which is just
a jacket fear puts on. The mare's sudden

stillness says look: fox. The world as ever
offering now distraction, now danger.
But no. How much I owe the trees, the hissing

raccoon outsmarting my heart. The shed
moving towards ruin in its own slow time.
There's something sprouting on the kitchen

table that's not supposed to. Everything
eager, rude and alive. Not just the knotweed
but the crows' hideous vowels; buds blasted

open or whipped young off the tree. Take your
pick: the ridge hurtling for the last rag of snow
or simply lifting off with the first smack of dawn.

RARELY TOUCHED OR TOUCHING

A decade of self-contained adds up to innocence.
What I bring richly to bed is evidence of the world;
when I wake it's just a just crib full of books, day
yawning forward with no mother in the next room
and again last night I forgot to touch myself into being
—rain on the skylight the only fingers not my own.
The tongue has given up on all but food. Unmoving,
moved is how I'm touched, from outside in, eyes
filling. What I have on my hands is my hands.

DREAMING WE

Try to fish back the tangible: kitchen, frame
of darkness speaking window, wood smooth
and non-insistent. Happy chatter a good dress,
nothing underneath.
                                Under dreams,
wish or fear; this one, wish—a seeping.

Under-silence like neon, the tiny pulsing, the not.
Under the question, the answer inside you all along.
Under a moment, music in filaments stopping. And him
on his feet saying, 'Here we are'
                            —*here* being nothing
                but the new word *we,* unspeakably present.

As in childhood: feeling the stirrups beneath
our feet, the ground beneath the horse, feeling
beneath the sky, above the fear.
                            Fear of *we*
we walk through with nothing under
(underground, as in childhood, nothing
        but wonder: worms, thunder-tunnels, China)
        —once all the things that would bring us here
do: two mouths of a certain age that have never kissed
                          like that.

        Sudden waking
so like sudden death in the hugeness
of what all did not just happen. Under bourbon,
smoke in the mountains.
Streaming, fugitive.

SPEAKING OF THE 3rd PERSON

Where is he? My teen-child was dependably
at home most nights, that made two of us.
Trees filed up & down the hill into forests.
The phone still sometimes rings; sometimes
I answer in my solo *sotto voce*. 'This is she'
always struck me as formal. And: if
anybody's asking, *she* no longer plays piano. *She*
does consider grammar. *She* is squinting believe
me forward.

SPEAKING OF GATES

Becoming she is, face cracked open mostly
pleasantly. New paint job, worn latches.
She hangs with Mr. Platonic until it hurts,
then goes it alone. Months pass. Miles.
March she drives spinning into ice muck,
but knows to call the tow truck. Meanwhile,
the prayer flags on the shed fade to perfect.
She may be ready to let you in. Nightly she
wonders: what looms between her and the
bloody meadow?

I WENT TO TEXAS TO BE TOUCHED

More or less. Like weather. Like the birds'
cawing in it. Like face to face with someone
you may have made up.
                          We are all at least
two people. I believe in the underside of leaves.
In the splinters inside the smooth wood and
the tough nubs' spunk. I believe in reality
like fog. Like yes no maybe. Like the mayoral
candidate who sent his twin to the parade.
He waved and waved.
                          Sometimes talking at all
is a lie. The more we lie, the less we believe.
Grapevines curl, grapes bleed. I vow to reach
no conclusions. So what if I think sandstorm,
you mudslide. If it's good, hurry. Or go slow.
Can we agree on gardening in the dark?
The folly of hastily-raised fences? A horizon
wide as ether?
                          All of the above. Above all, touching.
I believe I was.

WHO CAN SAY

The ferry draws me across the sound—a gentle yanking-
back to life alone—while a thread of clouds crosses
the moon, fat-yellow with glow. My face in the rear-view
suffers its path. Bound for home, no way not to ponder
the change that happens in our absence. Salty ropes sway
in the belly of the boat as night comes down. When gauze
cuts the moon precisely in half, I feel most myself, a fabric
divided. How did I miss the moment the sky gave up its blue
to meet dark water? Engine-roar is absorbed by the sky.
Inner overtures. We're slowing. Water on the hull is loud lace
as the moon makes its way to me over black tulle. I defy you
to paint this. If as I believe everything counts, there's more
of pleasure. After long none, there is a man—but who can say
who he is? Delicious, the fear the ocean holds in the dark.

BECAUSE WALKING

Because walking is a yielding, what to do but look?
In the frothy stream, a square-headed boy in waders,
full of purpose. Early onrush of violets knitting
the green. Lanky woman tra-la-la-ing, either impish
or loony, we can't know, but we wish her her wishes.
The earthworms are out in force, the dogwood newly

naked. Seeing—the first kind, vast and made of seed-
flash—brings us to our knees. Rage, too, can do this:
hammer and landslide, an exhilaration. Like a coyote's
release—ragged, tentative, then the cutting loose. What's
wrong with being called an outcry, a fearsome clanging
that marks not simply bruises but the long road, the map,

the map lost, the lost? The flit of what we can have?
And always there is the slow re-leafing, until one day
the window, the one we can't—no matter what—see into.
Time to lean back, shoulder-blades to shingles, slide
down and sit a bit in the dirt. Breathe in all that's left:
cellar damp and petal breath. Good to have come on foot.

DECADE PARADE

The Broker adored Hildegard of Bingen—
but was a pussycat like my ex before the X.
Flannel Shirt was into conspiracy theories
and Sportswriter wanted a wife bad—
and found one a couple weeks after I passed
on the job. Bob #2 had some cockamamie
ideas about harnessing sexual energy. I knew
he was right, but he so wasn't. Head of Hair
wore a retainer and funny underwear.
None of them could be called *Que Será* or
sidelong or had, to my knowledge, a tattoo.
One had a performance problem and resembled
Howard Dean (neither of which was the problem).
Junior partner had a head of hair, too, but Oh
so much blather. No, I am not a bitch and yes
have many flaws, but the old friend is way
too old a friend and the high school geek,
while handsome now, is still one. Three ex-wives
or permanently single, the whole lot of them
were too damned something. That slow food activist,
though, he saw through me in a way I don't yet
get. Which has me considering invisibility—
a counter-intuitive and possibly counter-
productive strategy, but maybe a good cover,
as I scan the crowd for a tattooed, bald
widower not named Bob, reluctant, loose-
limbed, and wearing linen, who gives good talk.

WOOD RUNS LOW

You could burn

picture frames, brown bags, that crutch
in the downstairs closet—watch your face
flush, your strain flash to ash and be gone.

Instead you layer up, worry which organ
has something bad brewing and is there time
for a new knot, a yes, something full-body?

(Ache, urge, curve of neck—these appear
strict outside the late window.) Shiver.
Look to find nerve in your nerves. Instruct

screws the house over to loosen, doorframes,
hand tools, counters to conceive coolish ease.
Turn your rocker from the lamplight eagerly

streaming its motes. Night's arms are open.
A slab of moonshine slaps across hearthstone.
These are your feet. You are perched not

buckled to this hill.

HE BRINGS WOOD

He brings wood, soup, family photos, dear nearness—and I remain
friendly but strange, waiting out dormancy, wishing for swoon. Once
upon a time was a woman, spreading but longing, set in her ways:
proud and unsure whether to take reluctance for weakness or
wisdom. The stars in night sky say what? On one hand, intensity
is distant; on the other, the Pleiades are a smudge only without
my glasses. Bird, good faithful bird, voluntarily, wooingly, in hand,
am I not grateful? Once upon a time was a loneliness—hypothetical
or real? Warm arm fallen to thigh, fingers drawn along the nape,
can they be welcomed? She could reveal her sins: love of surface,
betrayals of the body, fears of the bodily, an inventory of fault-lines
and hearth-quakes. Face to face with palpable, does she mean to deter
or solidify capture? Words open doors this woman I am seems ready for,
but to translate the mouth back to wordless, to flesh: must there be rapture?

COME HITHER

They say it's like willing yourself

                               I am the queen of wishing

well

                          Bathroom sinks want mirrors

to make the morning

                                        open

Set your shoulders back loosely
and your heart will stay

                        which may be a lie but I want it

open
             like I want someone who prefers winter stars

Street dark, hallway empty

               I make you up and ask: in your world,
November

                      leaves who insist on
                          hanging on,
What's that saying—

                  are they good little leaves
                       or naughty?
we get the love

              Woods is plural but trees so singular
we think we deserve—

                Bark and bark and bark
             but inside the wood the pith

and where does faith come from?
                   In grasses it's even hollow
It doesn't matter

               Strength I've learned is forever
               taking turns with weakness

Put in a call to the universe

                  I want water from down deep

full of laughter

                  I've had it with this always hallway

Be where and who you are

               More of me under than above-ground

He will turn up

                            like a turnip

underfoot

like a lovely stone

                         If you happen by
                             upend me

SPEAKING OF ORDER, SPEAKING OF SEX

Yes, no. Two adolescent magnolias each
dead center in crabgrass divided by
sidewalk: Yes and No, I named them,
walking daily down the middle. World
the color of capable. Ordered by doorbell,
fish tank, tithing—back when what we
did, clothed, was called petting. Naked
was not about to happen. Who really
remembers that gone self? Memory
morphed to depth-charge: magnolias
shedding soft screams.

SPEAKING OF NAKED

You've heard of the infamous emperor but are you aware of the commoners who pile on every last garment they own and pretend nakedness? Or those who peel off their clothes to hide their soul? We all fall for distraction now and again, but let us consider the truly naked. Maybe someone's approaching who is ready to be seen. Possibly in a mirror, we must wait and see. On the other hand we have the sleeping stone of a man someone scraped the moss off of—or the taunted line-up with bags over their heads. It's who does the disrobing and why. Oh our human tendrils. And what does the darling wisteria do all winter long?

SEE YOU

I'm sorry, I'm unable to give you my attention at this time.
I have an alphabet—I'd like to say nipping at my heels, but
it's playing dead. Worse, it's not all words, the lexicon

of what's catching up with me, cooling down: knees no longer
ever-ready to lift me from a squat; heart and brain—instead
of disputing ground—inclined to sit it out. Time to rehabilitate

the intentional mode! To swim in difference, I visit a city:
bone structures and complexions filling me and the train
with the idea of acceptance, followed by a litany of injuries

and certainties I have not yet met, followed by ones I have.
Yesterday is itself, thundering past behind smeared glass,
but I'm today, unable to befriend my own face. Being lost

is either not knowing which unfamiliar thing to notice
or being surrounded by so much familiar we can't see
the door. This is a map because I say so. You don't know me

yet, future last and lasting lover, I'm sitting on the stairs.
Pardon the riddles, and the wait. Wind, water, warmth.
When the mirror shows me a blossom, I'll see you.

WHERE A BIRD IS ALWAYS NESTING

For Adélia Prado & Zé Freitas

Fresh from a land where they eat
even the tough heart of the pineapple
because ripening in the dusty field it's

sunned to the core, tender-sweet like
the memory of a baby's face;
fresh from friends who trust me

in another language, spill into my lap
more fierce doubt and revel than ever
it has held; fresh from who I am there

where God is real and a bird is always
nesting in the grapevine, I land back
among my emblems of hands and palm

trees and ready irony, and see only
pebbles, and baubles and pace. Dutiful,
I sliver, I schedule, I chew the fat

of complaint, but my mind's on that
pineapple. It was small and sickly pale
and I was loved across every divide.

GOD OR NO GOD

Deer not clacking through snow crust
after apples, crows thankfully asleep,
coyotes whispering to young
not yet ready to test their pipes—
midnight is broken by my sump-pump
disgorging the day's melt-seep. Yes.
What can *I* do without?

The first time I rode the ambulance
there was a hole in someone's head.
Because all matter crumbles, because
chunk and mouth, bone of skull,
because this guy knew where to point.
That my hands did all the right things;
that he died as he meant to; that he made me
wildly alive—all true.

Ten years on, cumin seeds scorching in the pan
are my children, my slipknot, my go-to.
Because I believe myself fragrant
I am spitting me back out.
I renounce dog-eared and dog tired and even
dogged—no, dogged is good.
Because God or no god are both monstrous.
Because wrists don't age. Because kisses
or memories of kisses. Because
hull and *grave* equally ravish.

The first time I gave myself an eyelash of a chance
to change, it will be tomorrow, and luckily
I'm watching. Because let the tenses be scrambled.
The world happens momentarily.

Acknowledgments

Grateful acknowledgment is made to the journals and anthologies in which these poems first appeared, sometimes in earlier versions:

American Poetry Review: "Dreaming We," "The Person You Cannot Love," and "Yours, Lena"

Colorado Review: "Speaking of Rich"

Connotation Press: An Online Artifact, "Diminuet Feminina" and "Fireflies at the Altar"

Green Mountains Review: "Begonia Was Her Name-O," "Flood, According to Her," and "Flood, According to Him"

Never Before: Poems About First Experiences (Four Way Books, 2005): "First Sight"

Northern Woodlands: "Knot in Night Sky"

Orion: "Be Here First"

Prairie Schooner: "Late Love," "Decade Parade," and "He Brings Wood"

Tin House: "Ghazal for Shahid"

Deep and heartfelt thanks to Smith College, Peter and Margi Gregory, the Dorset Colony House, and Trinity University, San Antonio, for generous gifts of writing space and place; to Jeffrey Levine and Jim Schley at Tupelo for friendship, long labor, and acumen; to my brilliant posse of creative cohorts: Annie Boutelle, Amy Dryansky, Diana Gordon, Deborah Gorlin, Joan Houlihan, Maya Janson, Mary Koncel, Anne Marie Macari, April Ossmann, Carol Potter, Barbara Ras, and Martha Rhodes, whose poems and attentions buoy me; and to my father, whose unswerving love sustains.

Other books from Tupelo Press

This Lamentable City,
Polina Barskova, edited and
translated by Ilya Kaminsky

This Nest, Swift Passerine,
Dan Beachy-Quick

Cloisters,
Kristin Bock

Modern History:
Prose Poems 1987–2007,
Christopher Buckley

Stone Lyre: Poems of René Char,
translated, by Nancy Naomi Carlson

Spill,
Michael Chitwood

staring at the animal,
John Cross

Psalm,
Carol Ann Davis

Orpheus on the Red Line,
Theodore Deppe

Then, Something,
Patricia Fargnoli

Calendars,
Annie Finch

Other Fugitives & Other Strangers,
Rigoberto González

Keep This Forever,
Mark Halliday

Inflorescence,
Sarah Hannah

The Us,
Joan Houlihan

Red Summer,
Amaud Jamaul Johnson

Dancing in Odessa,
Ilya Kaminsky

Ardor,
Karen An-hwei Lee

Dismal Rock,
Davis McCombs

Biogeography,
Sandra Meek

Flinch of Song,
Jennifer Militello

At the Drive-In Volcano,
Aimee Nezhukumatathil

The Beginning of the Fields,
Angela Shaw

Selected Poems, 1970–2005,
Floyd Skloot

Human Nature,
Gary Soto

Nude in Winter,
Francine Sterle

Embryos & Idiots,
Larissa Szporluk

Archicembalo,
G.C. Waldrep

This Sharpening,
Ellen Doré Watson

The Book of Whispering
in the Projection Booth,
Joshua Marie Wilkinson

Narcissus,
Cecilia Woloch

American Linden,
Matthew Zapruder

Monkey Lightning,
Martha Zweig

See our complete backlist
at www.tupelopress.org